CONCRETE

From the Ground Up

CONCRETE

From the Ground Up

Larissa Theule

ILLUSTRATED BY

Steve Light

CANDLEWICK PRESS

CONCRETE is a composite building material.

Composite means made up of different parts.

The different parts that make up concrete are stone, sand, water, and cement.

STONE

SAND

WATER

LIMESTONE + CLAY
[CEMENT]

Cement is not the same as concrete.

Cement is a part of concrete and works as a glue to hold all the other parts together. Cement is typically made of limestone and clay. On its own, cement can be used for small jobs, like a front walkway, but it's too weak for big jobs. For big jobs, you need concrete.

Different recipes of stone, sand, and cement make different kinds of concrete.

Early makers of concrete used whatever naturally occurring resources and technology were available to them. Their concrete looked different from the concrete we use today.

This is Göbekli Tepe, in Turkey. It's the oldest-known holy site in the world. It dates to around 9600 BCE, thousands of years before humans even invented the wheel.

Among the many wonders of Göbekli Tepe's construction are these limestone T-shaped pillars, as well as this concrete-like flooring, the first of its kind, and rather fancy for its time.

For thousands of years, people used concrete-like materials in non-structural ways, like as mortar. Mortar is a plastic material that hardens when it dries and is often used to hold stone and brick together.

The Dadiwan culture of China used concrete-like material, as did the Minoans of Crete, the Nabataean Bedouins in Syria, and the Mayans in Mesoamerica, among others.

However, concrete wasn't used as a major structural building material until the Romans started to build.

Ancient Romans liked to build.

Roman concrete was extra-strong, and it could harden even under water because Romans used pozzolana in their cement. Pozzolana is volcanic ash. Italy has many volcanoes, and therefore lots of volcanic ash.

Because their concrete was extra-strong, Romans used it along with brick and stone to build large-scale structures such as aqueducts.

The Colosseum is another Roman structure made with concrete.

The Colosseum is an oval amphitheater that hosted grand, often bloody events.

It could seat more than fifty thousand people. Audiences could watch mock sea

battles, exotic animal shows, executions, chariot races, and gladiator fights.

Gladiators were trained fighters. Most were enslaved. They were made to fight each other and wild animals, sometimes to the death.

That gladiator's name is Flamma. He was famous for winning twenty-one times and was unique in that he liked being in the arena.

I'm Flamma. I love to fight!

Rome had many emperors.

One of Rome's emperors, Emperor Hadrian, commanded that a temple called the Pantheon be rebuilt with the greatest dome the world had ever seen. He insisted that the dome be made of concrete.

Everyone except Emperor Hadrian was nervous about building the Pantheon's dome.

Concrete has good *compressive* strength: you can put a lot of weight on concrete before it breaks. But concrete has poor *tensile* strength: when you stretch concrete, it becomes weak.

A concrete dome pushes both down and out, putting the concrete in compression and tension at the same time and placing considerable strain on the walls holding it up.

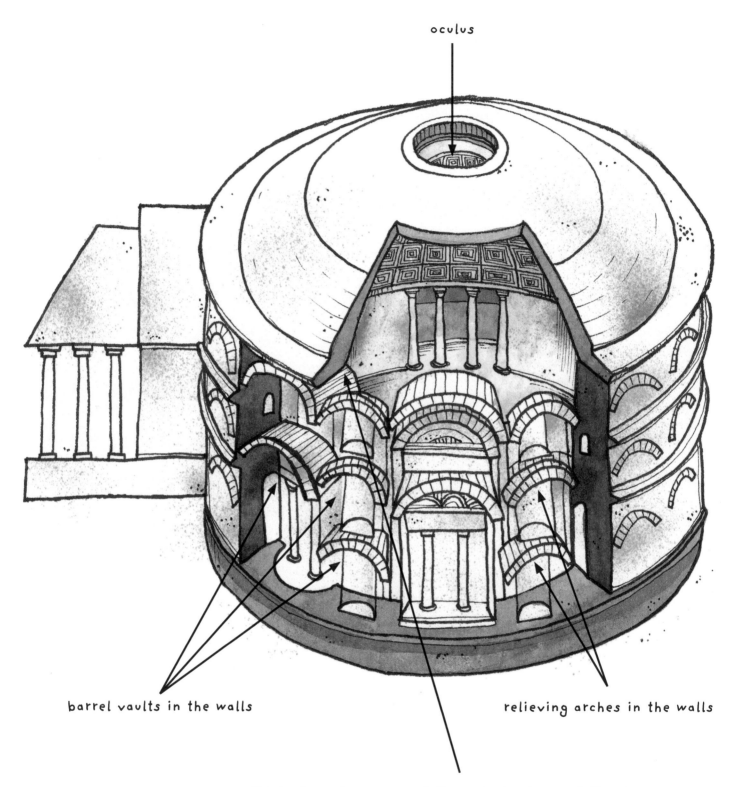

oculus

barrel vaults in the walls

relieving arches in the walls

thick ring of masonry at the exterior base of the dome

Engineers and masons used a few tricks to balance tension and compression forces in the structure. It was completed in 125 CE.

Two thousand years later, the Pantheon is still a marvel to behold.

After the fall of the Roman Empire, around 476 CE, the recipe for Roman concrete was lost.

Stone, however, continued to be used as a lasting, universal building material.

Monolithic means cut and chiseled from a single rock. That's right—one single rock.

In Ethiopia around the thirteenth century, King Lalibela ordered the construction of eleven monolithic churches, including the Church of Saint George.

In the fifteenth century, Incas built Machu Picchu in the Andes Mountains, most probably as a retreat for Incan emperors. Engineers and builders constructed Machu Picchu using precisely cut stone bricks.

Wow. That's some view.

It wasn't until the eighteenth century (more than a thousand years after the fall of the Roman Empire) that concrete reemerged as a major building material, thanks to a civil engineer named John Smeaton.

Smeaton coined the term *civil engineer*. That means he invented it.

A civil engineer is someone who designs bridges, roads, dams, and other public structures.

Here's how concrete reemerged and why: In the English
Channel, a reef called the Eddystone Rocks had been wrecking
ships for centuries. Sailors needed a lighthouse to help them
guide their ships through the treacherous waters.

So in 1698, an engineer named Henry Winstanley built the first Eddystone lighthouse. He built it all out of wood. It had a rough first year.

Winstanley rebuilt the lighthouse, again out of wood. It blew away in a storm, along with Winstanley and five other men.

In 1709, a silk merchant named John Rudyard built a new lighthouse, also out of wood. His lighthouse lasted fifty years, then caught fire and burned down.

Finally, the Royal Society of London for Improving Natural Knowledge hired John Smeaton, who happened to be a fellow of the society.

Based on the ash heap of evidence, Smeaton concluded that wood was not a good material for a lighthouse. He needed something much stronger.

He experimented with different mixtures of stone, sand, water, and cement. Using these readily available materials, he came up with a brand-new recipe for the ancient composite, concrete.

STONE

WATER

SAND

LIMESTONE   +   CLAY

[CEMENT]

What made Smeaton's recipe unique was that his cement was composed of a perfect proportion of limestone to clay that made it possible to harden under water.

In 1757, Smeaton began building a new Eddystone lighthouse using granite and concrete. In doing so, he reintroduced concrete to the world.

Because of Smeaton, concrete began to change the landscape of planet Earth forever.

Later, Smeaton's lighthouse had to be moved because the ground under it was no longer stable, but the lighthouse itself still stands, as sturdy as ever.

In time, engineers and architects wanted to use concrete for all sorts of projects. However, concrete's poor tensile strength limited their ambitions. If they stretched concrete, it would weaken.

In the 1860s, the problem was solved by the invention of reinforced concrete. Reinforced concrete is concrete with steel rods running through it.

Steel has good tensile strength.

Concrete has good compressive strength.

When used together,
anything seemed possible.

Things like concrete
towers that touch the sky.

This is the Ingalls Building.
It's the first reinforced
concrete skyscraper, built
in Ohio in 1903. It's sixteen
stories tall.

That reporter doesn't
trust reinforced
concrete. He's
convinced the building
will collapse during the
night. He's going to be
the first with the story.

Reinforced concrete enabled the construction of large-scale dams.
Dams block the natural flow of rivers, often to generate electricity and
regulate water supply for people living in nearby cities.

This is the Three Gorges
Dam, spanning the Yangtze
River in Hubei Province,
China. It's 7,661 feet (2,335
meters) long and was
constructed between 1994
and 2003.

This is Hoover Dam, spanning the Colorado River in Arizona and Nevada. It's 725 feet (221 meters) tall and was constructed between 1931 and 1936, during the Great Depression.

Many bridges also use reinforced concrete.

Hi! I'm Emilie. I'm crossing the bridge to visit my friend Matthieu. It's his birthday today. He's turning seven.
A lovely thing about bridges is that they bring people together.

Unlike bridges, walls are sometimes built to divide places and keep people apart.

After Germany's defeat in World War II, both the country and its capital, Berlin, were divided into western zones and eastern zones. After a clash between east and west in 1961 known as the Berlin Crisis, a barbed wire and reinforced concrete wall was built by those in power on the eastern side. It encircled the western zones to prevent people in East Germany from ever going to West Germany, even if they had family and friends there.

The Berlin Wall was actually two walls with a space between them.

Lots and lots of rabbits lived between the two walls.

Whole herds of happy hoppers!

Concrete is strong, but it can be broken, even smashed. On November 9, 1989, the German people on both sides of the wall were sick and tired of being divided. So they tore the Berlin Wall down. They left only a small part of it standing as a memorial to all those who had died trying to cross it.

By now, people are getting pretty good at using concrete.
They're even having fun with it.

Jørn Utzon designed the Sydney Opera House, in Australia, in
a way that made the concrete roofs resemble billowing sails.

Tadao Ando designed the 4x4 House, in Kobe, Japan. It stands on the edge of the sea and resembles a lighthouse.

Zaha Hadid designed the Heydar Aliyev Center, in Baku, Azerbaijan. Its innovative flowing design is meant to be a reflection of the people's imagination and hopes for the future.

In a blend of fun, beauty, and reflection, artist Nancy Holt installed four concrete cylinders in a cross shape out in the desert of Utah in the 1970s. This type of large-scale sculpture or installation is called land art. To some, Holt's *Sun Tunnels* are as beautiful as the Pantheon.

Each cylinder is 18 feet (5.5 meters) long.

People have used concrete for floors, temples, lighthouses, skyscrapers, dams, bridges, public spaces, houses, and art.

As our world and planet change, our needs will change. As our needs change, so too will our concrete.

The concrete we make today is not the same concrete we'll be making in fifty years. The concrete of the future will also be used in ways we haven't thought of yet—but maybe we can imagine.

BIBLIOGRAPHY

Ando, Tadao, and Jean-Marie Martin. "4x4 House by Tadao Ando." *Architecture Week*, June 15, 2011.
   http://www.architectureweek.com/2011/0608/design_1-1.html.

Andrews, Evan. "10 Things You May Not Know About Roman Gladiators." History.com, September 1, 2018.
   www.history.com/news/10-things-you-may-not-know-about-roman-gladiators.

Cartwright, Mark. "Maya Architecture." *World History Encyclopedia*, September 20, 2015. https://www
   .worldhistory.org/Maya_Architecture/.

"Chronicle of the Berlin Wall." Chronik Der Mauer (Chronicle of the Wall) website. www.chronik-der-mauer
   .de/en/.

Courland, Robert. *Concrete Planet: The Strange and Fascinating Story of the World's Most Common Man-Made
   Material.* Amherst, NY: Prometheus, 2011.

Giedion, S. *Space, Time, and Architecture: The Growth of a New Tradition.* Cambridge, MA: Harvard University
   Press, 1995.

Hearn, Kelly, and Jason Golomb. "Machu Picchu." *National Geographic*, May 2, 2008. www.national geographic
   .com/history/archaeology/machu-picchu-mystery/.

Heydar Aliyev Center website. https://heydaraliyevcenter.az.

"Hoover Dam Historical Information." U.S. Bureau of Reclamation. www.usbr.gov/lc/hooverdam/history
/storymain.html.

"Ingalls Building." American Society of Civil Engineers. www.asce.org/project/ingalls-building/.

Li Zuixiong, Zhao Linyi, et al. "Research on the Modification of Two Traditional Building Materials in Ancient
China." *Heritage Science*, August 21, 2013. doi.org/10.1186/2050-7445-1-27.

"Our Story." Sydney Opera House. www.sydneyoperahouse.com/our-story.html.

"Rock-Hewn Churches: Lalibela." UNESCO World Heritage Centre. https://whc.unesco.org/en/list/18/.

"Salginatobel Bridge." American Society of Civil Engineers. www.asce.org/project/salginatobel-bridge/.

Strebe, Matthew. "Göbekli Tepe: Discovering the World's Oldest Religious Site." *Popular Archaeology*,
September 12, 2017. popular-archaeology.com/article/gobekli-tepe-discovering-the-worlds-oldest
-religious-site/.

"Sun Tunnels." Holt/Smithson Foundation. holtsmithsonfoundation.org/sun-tunnels.

Vila, Bob. "Concrete and Cement: A Case of Mistaken Identities." BobVila.com. www.bobvila.com/articles
/cement-vs-concrete/.

Windmuller-Luna, Kristen. "The Rock-Hewn Churches of Lalibela." *Heilbrunn Timeline of Art History*, September
2014. http://www.metmuseum.org/toah/hd/lali/hd_lali.htm.

For Philip
LT

To my dad, who taught me to build
SL

■   ■   ■

First edition 2022

Library of Congress Catalog Card Number pending
ISBN 978-1-5362-1250-1

22 23 24 25 26 27 CCP 10 9 8 7 6 5 4 3 2 1

Printed in Shenzhen, Guangdong, China

This book was typeset in Bauer Grotesk.
The illustrations were done in pen and ink, watercolor, and ink splatter.

Candlewick Press
99 Dover Street
Somerville, Massachusetts 02144

www.candlewick.com